MEMORABLE MOMENTS

Selected Poems and
Other Writings

Other books by Sheri A. Sutton

And So It Is

The Light of Christmas

In Remembrance of Me

MEMORABLE MOMENTS

Selected Poems
and Other Writings

SHERI A. SUTTON

MEMORABLE MOMENTS

Selected Poems
and Other Writings

©Sheri A. Sutton 2016

Published by
Sheri A. Sutton
P.O. Box 22
Wichita Falls, Texas 76307
United States of America

www.sheriasutton.com

ACKNOWLEDGEMENTS

Acknowledgement is made to the editors of the following publications where the works listed first appeared:

A Book of the Year, Poetry Society of Texas, 2012, *You Walked Away*

Times Record News, Sunday Edition, April 5, 2015, *The Resurrecting Power of God*

Times Record News, Sunday Edition, May 3, 2015, *Precious Gift of Motherhood: Complete Love*

Times Record News, Sunday Edition, May 31, 2015, *Redeeming Power of Prayer*

Wichita Falls Literature and Art Review, Vol. V, 2011, *A View of the Canyon*

DEDICATION...

To the members of the Wichita Falls Poetry Society,
(Chapter of the Poetry Society of Texas),
who have welcomed me, inspired me,
encouraged me, and supported my
efforts to be a poet and an author.
Thank you!

TABLE OF CONTENTS

TABLE OF CONTENTS

*For I am full of words, and the spirit within me compels me;
inside I am like bottled-up wine, like new wineskins ready to burst.*

Job 32:18-19 (NIV)

PREFACE

In 2002, a friend invited me to a meeting of the Wichita Falls Poetry Society (WFPS). Because I was curious, I accepted the invitation. Little did I know that I was about to encounter a group of people that would open up a longing for creativity that I had not experienced before.

In my profession, I was always comfortable with developing presentations, reports, or other business information. I was an accountant by trade; and most of my professional writing, although perhaps somewhat creative at times, was certainly not poetic. Although I enjoyed reading the works of various poets, I had only dabbled sporadically over the years in writing anything that resembled a poem.

Even in school, I cringed when poetic writing was the desired outcome in a class. Perhaps, I was too afraid of others' reactions or failing the required assignment. Regardless, I had never anticipated studying or writing poetry on a regular basis.

As I continued with the WFPS, I experienced creativity at its best. The poets who assembled monthly wrote some of the most beautiful poems that I had ever read. Ordinary people produced something extraordinary because they tapped into their creative consciousness on a regular basis.

At the monthly meetings, we studied form, meter, styles, poets, and various other topics related to poetry. We submitted our poems on a monthly basis to be judged and critiqued by poets throughout the state. Occasionally, we would have a guest poet who would read poetry or teach us something new and challenging. Other times, several in our group did public readings. It was all these types of activities that propelled me to attempt to write.

Poetry gives us a way to express what we often cannot express in conversation. Although poetry is developed through our own experiences, or perhaps our perceived experiences, it exposes an intimacy that we cannot bear otherwise.

1

Of course, poetry is subjective. We do not all like the same. Sometimes the poet has one destination in mind, and the reader arrives at another. Often times, the content of the poem does not resonate with the reader. However, poetry often speaks to us when nothing else does. It connects us to mankind and asks us to recognize and accept the human condition in all of us.

Since that fateful day in 2002, I have written many poems—some good, some not so good, and some still a work in progress. I have included in *Memorable Moments* those that I believe to be the best to date. The 19th century French novelist, Gustave Flaubert, once stated, "There is not a particle of life which does not bear poetry within it." Consequently, this book examines different aspects of our human experience using poetic form as well as other writings. It is my humble hope that these offerings will touch you, the reader, on a very basic and personal level.

I believe that we all have a creative spirit inside of us waiting to be set free. We may not all be poets or writers, but we all have that inherent ability to imagine something wonderful and beautiful. Take the risk and open yourself up to that artistic force. You will be glad you did.

Sheri A. Sutton

FAITH AND FAMILY

Faith is an important ideal in American culture, perhaps in all cultures. Faith in something greater than ourselves helps us to keep moving forward even when all seems impossible. Faith gives us hope—hope for a better outcome, hope for a better tomorrow, and ultimately hope for deliverance from our human failings. Without hope, there is no progress, only struggle and disappointment.

Since the beginning of time, people have pondered the mysteries of the universe. Is there a creator that out of nothing created the world and all therein? Is there something beyond ourselves that gives life, light, and love? Is there a purpose in all things? Is there eternal life after death? Thousands of possible answers to thousands of questions depend on which book we read, philosopher we study, or our own personal experiences.

But one might surmise that those who practice a faith are more likely to view the world differently than those who do not. Possibly, it is faith that gives us the strength and courage to live in today's world. Perhaps, faith moves us from the ordinary into the extraordinary. And maybe, just maybe, faith is the catalyst that propels us to some higher purpose in life. Regardless what each of us believe, our beliefs create our lives.

Living in community with one another has been paramount in the success of any culture. Family is where community begins. Family beliefs, traditions, rituals, and values create an atmosphere for success or failure. And what we learn within our families, we take into the world.

The family environment can be healthy and productive or sadly, as in some cases, unhealthy and destructive. When we experience a family that provides, nurtures, and creates an atmosphere of acceptance, belonging, and well-being, we are then equipped to be a part of creating a better world.

Thousands of poems, books, and articles have been written concerning faith and family, and thousands more will be written. Perhaps, it is the poet's purpose to give us a way to view our ideals so that we can identify, savor, mourn, and reconcile to our own individual experiences. When we find our commonality instead of looking for our differences, the world becomes a healthier environment for everyone.

Awaken

As the porch swing gently sways, I sit comfortably still
and witness the North Texas morning come alive.
Though daily temperatures will soar over 100 degrees,
the morning breeze feels almost cool as it caresses my face.

The sun creeps over the horizon to announce the dawn.
Sprinklers water lawns to give a much-needed drink,
and blades of grass appear to raise their heads in thankfulness.
Sunflowers, periwinkles, and begonias bathe in the sunlight.

Cardinals, blue jays, and sparrows dive toward the birdbath,
each hoping to get the first splash of the morning.
Lying by my feet, our dog quietly surveys the surroundings
and waits patiently for the first squirrel to make an appearance.

Peace surrounds me. I close my eyes and am filled with gratitude.
My spirit awakens as I sit in the stillness.
I slowly breathe in and out, consciously aware
that a powerful creative energy brings life to me.

A loving power surrounds me with its gentle embrace.
Energized and empowered, I breathe deeply one more time.
A squawking mockingbird breaks the silence—
I open my eyes and rise to tackle the chores of the day.

Woman

Who is woman?

She is—
>a mother, teacher, lover, friend
>the guttural scream when loving, birthing, grieving
>the muse when dancing, singing, creating

She laughs, cries, teases, feeds, nurtures, heals

She is—
>wisdom, strength, power
>a smile, a touch, a kiss, a whisper
>beauty, grace, and time eternal

Who is woman?

I am!

Super Heroes

Superman—faster than a speeding bullet;
swift to help someone in need
or save Metropolis from disaster.

Batman, the Cape Crusader,
battling throughout the night
to rescue Gotham City from evil villains.

Two super heroes ready at a moment's notice
to leap tall buildings, outsmart evil,
and save the world from total destruction.

In real life, brothers pretending to be
but dreaming that someday, in some way,
they might truly save the world.

Thank You

In a simple thank you note my granddaughter wrote,
"I love you and Christmas." I laughed as
my heart filled with joy and my eyes with tears.

She had fun that week making Krispie Treats,
playing softball, and watching Mary Poppins.
We rode the trails rescuing princesses
and picnicked in the park with the big slide.

Little brother paid no mind. He went about his business,
happy to be outdoors, free to run and explore.
The week was delightful and much too short as always.

"Thank you in my heart," she ended the note.
I smiled at the simplicity and the wisdom of those words.
Soon they will come again to run, play, and explore—
each visit bringing treasured memories for us to share.

The Choice

The rain is cold against my face;
My teardrops fall without a trace.
With fear I walk throughout the night.
Where is the hope? Where is the light?

I walk along the empty street;
I hear no sound of passing feet.
Alone am I without a friend.
Can this be all? Is this the end?

No ending to this long dark night;
With fear I march straight to the fight.
So will I win or will I lose?
The choice is mine, and I must choose.

I stumble, fall, and rise again;
My body's weak. I feel the pain.
The day dawns bold with all its might.
This is the hope. This is the light.

Change Your Heart

Look up into the azure sky
And watch a lonely eagle fly.
Drink in its beauty, watch it soar—
Your heart will change for evermore.

Or watch your baby while she sleeps;
Imagine all the dreams she keeps.
Give your blessing so she can soar—
Your heart will change for evermore.

Release your fears and doubts today
And know a freedom as you pray.
Become the eagle, you will soar—
Your heart will change for evermore.

I Give You My Life

"Be still, and know that I am God." Psalm 46:10 (NIV)

In the silence of this room,
I feel your presence.
It fills my soul and
Becomes my very essence.

Kneeling quietly to pray,
I give you my love.
I offer my will,
And feel your smile from above.

> I give you my life
> In the silence of this moment.
> I give you my life
> Without a single word spoken...

I commit my life fully
As I heed your call.
Blessed by endless grace,
May I ever give my all.

> I give you my life
> In the silence of this moment.
> I give you my life
> Without a single word spoken...

The Resurrecting Power of God

With the arrival of seasonal temperatures and recent rains, daffodils, tulips and wildflowers push through the unyielding soil of winter and lift their heads. Trees are in full bloom and birds are building nests for the birth of their young. All around us is the dynamic energy of life.

Today is Easter Sunday and Christians around the world celebrate the risen Christ. Over 2,000 years ago, God came to earth to be in a relationship with his people as he had never been before. As Jesus, the Son of God and the Son of Man, he walked among his creation and shared with them the meaning of life, love, truth, forgiveness and mercy. Many followed him, but many despised him and conspired against him. One of his own disciples betrayed him, and religious leaders falsely accused and convicted him. He was crucified and his broken body laid in a cold stone tomb.

Many thought that was the end of the story, but with God there is always more to the story. The chains of death were broken, and Jesus the Christ and long awaited Messiah was raised from the abyss of darkness into the eternal light. That resurrecting power of God is still available for us today.

We all have those moments in our lives when we are filled with anguish, despair or grief so overpowering that we plunge into a pit of darkness. Perhaps we have regrets about the choices we have made or at times feel unloved and unwanted. Maybe we suffer from the loss of loved ones or the loss of long sought after dreams. We may endure persecution and ridicule for our beliefs or life styles. Life is unfair and often cruel and devastating. But God's resurrecting power can transport us from the depths of our brokenness to restoration and wholeness.

The whole of Christianity hinges on the resurrection. When Jesus was crucified, he took all the burdens of the world, all our sins and shortcomings and all the despair and anguish of our lives to the depths of darkness and returned in the fullness of glory. In that eternal moment of redemption, he disarmed everything of this world that claims authority over humanity. He gave us the chance for new life. He gave us the chance to begin again. He gave us hope.

Hope fuels the possibility of healing, change and transformation. Hope propels us forward even when we are weary and burdened from the struggles of life. At any moment the power of God as witnessed through the resurrection of Jesus Christ can transform our lives. When we are dead in spirit, that power can renew us and raise us from the tomb of sorrow and misery into the light of the living God.

Against all odds a flower pushes its way through the deadness of winter and lifts its head toward the light, and God's world once again comes alive. Soon the ashen color of winter's landscape will be a memory, and the vibrant palette of spring will paint our daily lives. On this Easter morning, we have the opportunity to reaffirm our faith and belief in the risen Christ and know with assurance that absolutely nothing is impossible with God.

LIFE AND LOVE

As recorded in Genesis 2:7, God "breathed into his nostrils the breath of life, and the man became a living being." In one divine moment in time, life pulsed through our bodies. We could breathe, we could love, we could hate, we could create, and we could destroy. Life began, and we had the choice to accomplish great things or to be complacent and indifferent.

Life is compelling. It is comprised of everyday experiences that continue to change us and transform us. Life can be easy, or it can be difficult. It can be fun and interesting, or it can be labor intensive and boring. It can lead us down a path of enlightenment or into the abyss of despair. Life gives us no guarantees, only possibilities dependent on our own imaginations.

It is often said that life is a journey, not a destination. Often, we are so fixated on where we want to go that we miss the magical moments and happenings along the way. We are meant to enjoy and savor every moment in our lives, to live life fully with imagination and wonder, and to open ourselves to unlimited potential.

Much has been written about love, and it is certain that much more will be written. We have all experienced love in some form or another. Many of us have enjoyed the faithful love of a spouse, the love of children and grandchildren, and the love of friendship. Some of us have suffered the pain of a broken heart when love ended unexpectedly. Love can be the most joyful experience of our lives, or it can take us to a place of regret and grief.

Poetic writing has a way of communicating the universal complexities of love in such a way that all of us can identify or connect on some level of understanding because of our own encounters. Perhaps, poetry brings us to a deeper awareness of the struggle between the longing to receive love and the need to give love.

The poems and other writings included in this section are a sampling of thoughts that we might have in any twenty-four hour period of our lives. There are no great discoveries or new theories on the mysteries of life or the power of love listed here—just ideas to ponder in the middle of an ordinary day.

The Energy of Life

Boldly creating—
the hands of a lover,
powerful yet tender

Gently breathing—
the tides against the shore,
ebbing and flowing

Always sustaining—
a mother with her child,
feeding and nurturing

Ever changing—
the colors of the seasons,
dynamic yet subtle

Never ending—
the evolution of man,
transforming and ongoing

A Moment of Light

We are only a moment of light—
see the firefly's flicker on a summer's eve,
amazing yet ordinary
small but significant

Glorious beyond measure—
like the heavens on a clear night,
beautiful yet frightening
infinite but limited

We are only a moment of light—
see the flash of lightning zig-zag to earth,
defined yet changeable
powerful but inadequate

Splendor waiting to unfold—
like the rose opening slowly on a stem,
breathtaking yet subtle
living but dying

We are only a moment of light—
see the falling star against the sky,
brilliant yet fading
temporary but eternal.....

Adaptation

Choices and consequences play out
with no script or cue cards,
only speculation of the next word or action

Unknown characters, random encounters, and unexpected events
fill the scenes of one's existence,
bringing joy or pain depending on one's circumstances

Participants and spectators alike
wait with anticipation for the final act—
will there be joy, sadness, resolution, or death?

One's life lived in seconds, minutes, and hours;
continuous unrehearsed and unrepeated moments
to be celebrated and mourned each day

You Walked Away

It's not the first time you have walked away;
So many times you've walked away before.
To find another love from yesterday,
Again you choose to leave my life once more.
My heart is aching as I watch you leave,
An outpouring of tears begins to fall.
How can you leave so easily? I grieve.
Your loving words misled me after all.
Although, my dear, our tragic love is through,
I know in time my pain will fade away;
And I will face tomorrows free of you
Believing I will love another day.

I slowly close the door as you depart.
You were the deepest beat within my heart.

Forever Love

(1)

Flowing white gown shimmered in the candlelight,
and her face glowed with a soft radiance.
Taking his arm, she kissed her father's cheek.

Slow steps down the aisle calmed her excitement.
Behind her lay the past; before her, the future.
Life changed that day.

Her eyes filled with tears, and love stopped her heart.
Handsome and tall, dressed in his new black suit,
he waited for her.

Gazing deeply into each other's eyes,
they purposely pledged their love
and sealed it sweetly with a kiss.

Congratulations and best wishes filled the air,
when the happy couple left the church
to begin their life together.

(2)

She sets their wedding picture on the table.
Memories flash through her mind
as she recalls the many years they shared.

The image staring from the mirror reminds her.
Her silver hair glistens in the light;
she deliberately straightens her black dress.

Slow steps down the aisle calm her fears.
Still and peaceful he lies there
dressed in a new black suit.

Tears flood her eyes as
"Amazing Grace" fills the sanctuary.
Life will change today.

Leaning down, she kisses his cheek
while tenderly touching his hand.
"I'll love you forever," she whispers.

Precious Gift of Motherhood: Complete Love

Being a mother is no easy task. It has sometimes been referred to as "the hardest job you'll ever love." It requires long days, sleepless nights, patience, discipline and most importantly love. There are hundreds of books on the subject of motherhood, but until you are actually a mother do you fully understand the intense responsibility and ultimately the reward.

I am fortunate that I had a mother who loved me and whom I loved and admired. Although she died 26 years ago, I still want to call her and share what is happening in my life. Even now I visualize her in the kitchen cooking or baking, taking care of me when I was ill, or teaching me to sew. Of course, we had those stressful moments like most mothers and daughters, which prompted me to tell my daughter when she was young that we would not always agree or like one another. She confidently told me that we would always be friends! I am certain that we were not friends through junior high and part of high school. Thankfully those years passed and we survived.

Throughout motherhood there are those defining moments when nothing else matters except the love you have for your child. One such moment happened when my daughter was three years old. It was Mother's Day weekend, and her Grandma took her shopping. I was told that my daughter was on a mission to find the perfect gift. She looked and looked until she spied a yellow wire basket full of pink begonias. She handed the cashier her piggy bank and watched as the woman counted the coins that scattered across the counter. Early the next morning my daughter tiptoed into my room and carefully placed a bag beside the bed. "Happy Mommy's Day," she whispered.

I have never loved so much as in that moment. Not because of the gift, but because of the giver. That is what mothers do...love completely. God's gift of grace is much the same. He loves us—not because of what we do, but because of who we are. 1 John 3:1 states, "How great is the love the Father has lavished on us, that we should be called the children of God!" As God loves us so we are called to love one another, and there is no greater human love than a mother's love for her child.

My daughter is now the mother of three children. Her children are young and there are many years ahead to experience the sweetness and sadness of motherhood. I marvel at her patience and love for her family as well her unwavering commitment to their well being. Her children are incredibly fortunate.

Next Sunday is Mother's Day, an American holiday first celebrated in 1908. Anna Jarvis led the campaign to have a day of special recognition to honor her mother and all mothers as "the person who has done more for you than anyone in the world." Maybe this person in your life is your birth mother, perhaps an adoptive mother or a mentor who has greatly influenced who you are today.

So take a moment this week to remember, to make a call, to send a card or to plan a visit with the woman who loves you more than you can possibly imagine.

Daydreaming

I lie drowsily on a blanket
and enjoy the warmth of the sun.
I gaze deeply into the morning sky.

Various forms and shapes appear
as the clouds come alive.
I contemplate their images.

Many thoughts pervade my mind—
family, career, retirement
remind me of pending obligations.

The sun warms my face;
the soft grass cushions my body.
I close my eyes to block the sun.

My mind races with excitement—
school, friends, dances
fill my head with possibilities.

First love calls my name;
life seems full of promise.
I feel unafraid and powerful.

But age catches up,
and youth is a mere memory.
Life moves forward.

I ponder the passing of time;
then, I accept the truth—
child-like innocence is gone.

I lie drowsily on a blanket
and enjoy the warmth of the sun.
I gaze deeply into the morning sky.

Life's Good

Golden stalks of wheat blowin' in the wind, while the fur
on my back ruffles in the breeze and the sun warms my nose

as I stretch—and yawn.

Over in the pasture Mo and Buddy are grazin'.
I 'member when I'd round those boys up for supper,
but these days they mosey to the barn without much help.

Lying here on the porch, I keep my eye on things.
I might chase a squirrel, maybe two, or rabbits on a good day;
mostly I just watch the one who loves me workin' the place.
We're both gettin' a little slow though and do more sittin' than
workin'.

The evenin' comes as the sky becomes a pinkish-orange glow,
and another day ends as the full moon begins to rise.
Slowly he rocks the porch swing back and forth. It gently creaks.

"Cotton, ol' girl," he says, "don't get much better than this."
I cock my ear in agreement...

then stretch—and yawn. Life's good!

NATURE AND NURTURE

Nature, in its broadest sense, is the natural, physical, or material world or universe. Look around. Nature is everywhere. Majestic mountains, rolling plains, lakes and rivers, endless oceans, infinite space, birds of the air, creatures of the sea, and animals and vegetation of all types and species comprise our natural environment. Since the beginning of time, mankind has tried to understand and control all of nature.

Not only does nature offer us information to understand the mysteries of the world and mankind's position in it, but also it connects us to something greater than ourselves. We are all a part of something that goes beyond our comprehension, that in some cases is unexplainable, and that moves us to an appreciation of this world in which we live.

There is something innate in all of us that identifies with nature. Dig in the dirt, smell the richness, and feel the fertility. Stand on the water's edge and listen to the ocean waves pound against the sandy shore. Gaze into the night sky and ponder the extent of the universe. When we spend a moment of reflection on our connection to nature, something happens.

Nature has a way of nurturing our spirits. When we are hurting, we can find solace in its beauty. When we are unhappy, we can find joy in the birth of new growth after a long, dreary winter. And when we are happy, nature celebrates with us in its array of colors, textures, and sounds that only increases our level of happiness and well-being.

But nature can also be violent and destructive. Tornadoes rage across the central plains, hurricanes flood the cities along the coastal shores, and years of drought and distress on the earth cause death and decay. And many times rebirth and restoration may take years. Nature can be our friend, but it can be our enemy as well.

The offerings in this section give us a look into the different aspects of nature and its ability to nurture our minds, bodies, and spirits. Something as simple as a baby rabbit or as majestic as the Grand Canyon gives us pause to ponder the wonders of this incredible world in which we live. Listen to the sounds, imagine the landscapes, and visualize the moment that gave birth to a poet's idea.

A View of the Canyon

Sitting on the porch of the El Tovar, I ponder the majesty and mystery of the Grand Canyon. The various strata come alive with color as sunlight and shadow dance along the canyon wall. A group of tourists carefully maneuvers mules down into the canyon, and I wonder if they appreciate early explorers who patiently paved the way.

A crow's caw breaks the silence. I squint my eyes;

the crow glides with ease,
quickly turning on his back—
above the shadows

With swift precision, it flips and swoops to lunch on unsuspecting prey. My eyes return to the canyon walls. Their appearance has altered in one miraculous moment. With reverent awe, I marvel at the incomparable beauty of God's creation.

Baby

Little black button eyes peer over the grass.
Two brown ears, still and erect, listen—
motionless, baby rabbit waits patiently.

I watch in awe of its natural instinct.
A perceived threat requires stillness,
so baby waits as if frozen in time.

Carefully, I slowly and quietly inch closer.
Eyes move, tiny nose twitches, and
baby rabbit scampers out of reach to safety.

I smile and go inside to finish the chores of the day.
Little black button eyes peer out from under the porch;
cautiously, baby moves into the soft, green grass.

Texas Summer

Another summer day begins—

tall grasses sway, baby birds feed, and horses graze in pastures.
The beauty of the Texas morning disguises the cruelty of the
afternoon.

> daisies raise their heads
> welcoming the morning sun—
> comfort will fade soon

It's a hot, lazy day. I sit on the porch and watch sweat beads run
down my ice tea glass. Traffic sounds in the distance promise travel
to a cooler place.

I sip my tea.

> afternoon sun burns
> critters seek shade from grim heat—
> scorched air hangs heavy

Dusk comes finally, and moderate relief is welcomed. I scan the sky
for hints of needed rain but see no promise of showers.

> colorful sunsets
> adorn Texas evening skies—
> parched land rests at night

Redeeming Power of Prayer

Since October 2010, most of Texas has experienced severe drought conditions. As the drought worsened, people began to pray. "Pray for rain" signs appeared in numerous yards across town, many participated in community prayer services and ministers included the ongoing drought in sermons and congregational prayers. As a result, our community has witnessed firsthand the power of prayer. During these last few weeks, we have received record amounts of rainfall in Wichita Falls and the surrounding area.

As we were praying for rain, we were also developing ways to conserve. Many installed systems to harvest rain water as well as grey water so that trees, flower beds and yards could be moderately irrigated. Non-indigenous plants and grasses were replaced by native grasses and plants, and hardscape beds made their entrance into the area's landscape.

While the citizens cut water consumption by greater numbers than predicted, our city leaders were busy designing and implementing a water reuse system. After months of effort and approval by the TCEQ, the water reuse project became a reality. This system adds millions of gallons of water daily to our supply.

But most importantly we prayed. We are a community built on faith. Through many previous challenges and disasters, we came together for the greater good of the whole community. Even on a daily basis, we reach beyond ourselves to give to those in need. The drought situation was no exception. We did what had to be done, and we prayed. And then the remarkable happened. The rains came.

Prayer is an extraordinary force. Not only does it connect us to a power beyond ourselves, it changes our perspective. As a community we became mindful of a greater good...conserving instead of wasting. Prayer is also redeeming. It makes a situation better and brings healing and restoration. After weeks of unprecedented rainfall, our lakes and rivers are abundantly full. The parched land drinks with abandon, and trees and plants once more flourish and grow.

But with great victory often comes great destruction. Farmers watched as record-setting rains damaged crops. Severe flooding required the evacuation of hundreds of families from their homes, and emergency centers were set up at various locations to help those displaced. Countless volunteers filled sand bags to keep flood waters at bay in the most vulnerable areas.

So what do we do now? We come to the aid of our neighbors. We provide where there is a need. We lend a helping hand, a shoulder to cry on or a home cooked meal. But most importantly we pray. Pray with gratitude for the needed rain. Pray for the farmers who have lost their crops. Pray for those who return to their homes to cleanup or rebuild. Pray for our citizens who persevere in their conservation efforts. And pray for our city leaders who continue to develop water saving plans for our community.

God heard our pleas for water. He will hear our pleas for healing. "Do not be anxious about anything, but in every situation, by prayer and petition, with thanksgiving, present your requests to God" (Philippians 4:6).

Fall Comes Quietly

Days grow short, and morning dew glistens on grass blades as the landscape color pallet fades slowly into autumn. Birds in formation begin their journeys to warmer climates as Monarch butterflies, a beautiful fall surprise, visit briefly before continuing their southern migration.

> fall comes quietly,
> October winds blow gently—
> leaves rustle all day

Savoring a simple picnic lunch, I watch sunbeams gleaming from the western sky dance through the pecan trees. The sunlight warms my body and refreshes my soul as the hammock swings and tenderly rocks my sleepy spirit.

Too soon, my weekend respite ends. Healing peacefulness fills my spirit as I walk home. Fallen leaves crackle beneath my footsteps.

> evening sun sets now—
> colors of red, orange, pink
> stretch across the sky

Crisp evening air, promising winter's approach, requires a jacket for warmth. Brilliant stars illuminate the dark infinite vastness of the night sky as the harvest moon teases my empty hammock. I smile. Memories of today will be revisited in the weeks ahead.

The First Winter Snow

Hush, listen—long-awaited snow begins to fall.
As delicate lacey flakes swish softly through the air,
a winter's night magically transforms.

Moonbeams twinkle in the night sky
and dare snow crystals to glisten and glow.
In the cold mist, snowflakes dance to nature's rhythm.

Children turn and twirl amidst the snow flurries.
Wonder fills their faces and joy lights their eyes
when falling flakes touch their tongues with cold.

There is a quiet stillness as the ground turns white
and icicles sparkle on tree branches.
The world seems to stop for this wintry miracle.

Peacefulness fills the air to remind us—
escape from this chaotic, frenzied world
may be found when awed by the first winter snow.

It's Christmas Eve

It's Christmas Eve and soft snow is falling,
The ground's covered in a blanket of white.
The angel voices are sweetly calling
On this glorious, wondrous, silent night.

The ground's covered in a blanket of white
Under the glistening light of the moon.
On this glorious, wondrous, silent night
The world will be a white wonderland soon.

Under the glistening light of the moon,
The angel voices are sweetly calling.
The world will be a white wonderland soon.
It's Christmas Eve and soft snow is falling.

Another Winter Day

Days are cold and nights even colder since winter has arrived.
Each day dawns boldly announcing its weather forecast
with blustery winds and icy crystals on blades of dead grass.

With a second cup of coffee, cozy in front of the wood stove,
I read morning meditations and plan the day.
Dreaming dog dreams, Cotton lies beside my feet.

The wind blows relentlessly sending shivers up my spine
as I feed the horses, chip ice in water troughs, and muck stalls.
When chores are finished, the warm house offers welcomed relief.

I sit at the computer and gaze at the wheat field through the
window. Ideas, words, sounds, and visions begin to fill my mind.
My fingers touch the keys, and the writing begins.

AFTERWORD

Plato is quoted as saying, "Poetry is nearer to vital truth than history." If vital truth is defined as the most fundamental of principles that identify man and the society in which he lives, then vital truth reaches beyond history. Vital truth is at the core of ideas, emotions, or feelings that poetic writing exposes.

Poetry can speak for us when we cannot find the words to speak for ourselves. It can define our innermost thoughts and dreams. And it can take us on an internal journey to the deepest part of our spirits where we can discover the truth of who we are.

The poetry and writings included in this book are ordinary moments that are common events one might experience on any average day. But upon further review, they are not ordinary moments—they are memorable moments that define us.

Most of us are guilty of missing those moments that bring meaning, joy, surprise, or truth. We are too busy in the hustle and bustle of everyday living to stop and recognize the one essential truth—we are to live fully awake in every moment.

As you read through *Memorable Moments*, perhaps you felt the wonder of the first winter snow, cried over a lost love, or appreciated the power of faith. Maybe you visualized yourself within the words and descriptions. Or perhaps you identified with the writer in an unexpected and surprising way.

Ordinary, memorable moments expand our humanity and open our hearts to a greater awareness and understanding of ourselves and the world in which we live. Most importantly, those moments give us a glimpse of who we are and a hint of who we can be.

ABOUT THE AUTHOR

Sheri A. Sutton is an author, devotional writer, and poet. *Memorable Moments,* her fourth book, offers selected poems and other writings that focus on the moments in our lives that give meaning to the ordinary and transform us.

As a member of the Wichita Falls Poetry Society and the Poetry Society of Texas, Sutton has been recognized in various contests. Her poetry has been published in the *Wichita Falls Literature and Art Review* magazine, The Poetry Society of Texas' *A Book of the Year,* and *Lifting the Sky.*

Sutton has written three devotional books; and, in addition, her devotional writing has been published in the *Secret Place* devotional magazine and the *Lenten Devotions on the Lord's Prayer.*

For a limited time, she wrote a monthly newspaper column while serving on the Community Editorial Board of the Times Record News.

Sutton also offers professional services that include writing and editing for books, newsletters, and other materials for individuals, companies, or organizations. Visit her website, www.sheriasutton.com, for more information.

Sutton and her husband, Lloyd Mark Sutton, live in Wichita Falls, Texas.

The Wichita Falls Poetry Society's regular meetings are held every third Saturday from September through May excluding December. The meetings are from 2:00-4:00p.m. in the Texas Room at the Kemp Center for the Arts, 1300 Lamar Sreet., Wichita Falls, Texas.

Made in the USA
Columbia, SC
30 June 2023

19742818R00033